THE HOW AND WHY WONDER F...
INSECTS

By RONALD N. ROOD

Illustrated by CYNTHIA and ALVIN KOEHLER

Editorial Production: DONALD D. WOLF

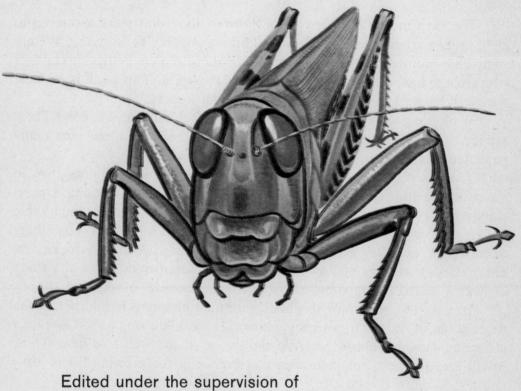

Edited under the supervision of

Dr. Paul E. Blackwood
Washington, D. C.

Text and illustrations approved by

Oakes A. White
Brooklyn Children's Museum
Brooklyn, New York

WONDER BOOKS • NEW YORK
A Division of GROSSET & DUNLAP, Inc.

Introduction

We learn in this *How and Why Wonder Book* that there are seven to eight million kinds of insects. How could there possibly be so many? We are sometimes prompted to ask the same thing about the curiosities of children who seem to have endless questions about their world. This book is an ideal source of answers to children's questions about insects.

What is a gold bug? What is a water penny? What is an ant cow? These are just a few of the unusual insects described in the book, along with many more familiar ones.

There is perhaps no more remarkable change in living things than in the development of certain insects from egg to larva to pupa to adult. Understanding this process gives a person a deep appreciation for the remarkable patterns in nature. Seeking accurate descriptions of such patterns is one thing scientists do, and they get great personal satisfaction when they make new discoveries. This book may encourage some children to continue the study of insects, called *entomology,* and select this science as a vocation.

Parents, too, will enjoy this book with their children. In addition to the descriptions of insects, it gives suggestions for an interesting hobby — insect collecting. How to collect, preserve and display them is all told here. Thus, it will prove to be a valuable science reference in the growing list of *How and Why Wonder Books.*

Paul E. Blackwood

Dr. Blackwood is a professional employee in the U. S. Office of Education. This book was edited by him in his private capacity and no official support or endorsement by the Office of Education is intended or should be inferred.

Contents

The Adult Insect

Is a spider an insect? How about a centipede or scorpion? Are crabs and lobsters really big insects that live in the water? Maybe you have seen a tick on a dog, or tiny red mites on plants. Are they insects?

How can you tell an insect from other creatures?

To find the answer, let's look at a good example of an insect — the butterfly. Think of the ways in which the butterfly is different from a spider. First, there are the big wings. Of all the crawling creatures, only insects have wings. Although spiders may sometimes sail through the air at the end of a long, thin, silk thread, like a parachute, no spider can really fly.

Count the number of legs on a butterfly. You'll find that there are six legs. A spider has eight. Crabs and lobsters have ten. Other creatures may have even more. But an insect has just six legs as an adult. Some baby insects seem to have too many legs. Others, like fly maggots, seem to have none at all.

How many legs does an insect have?

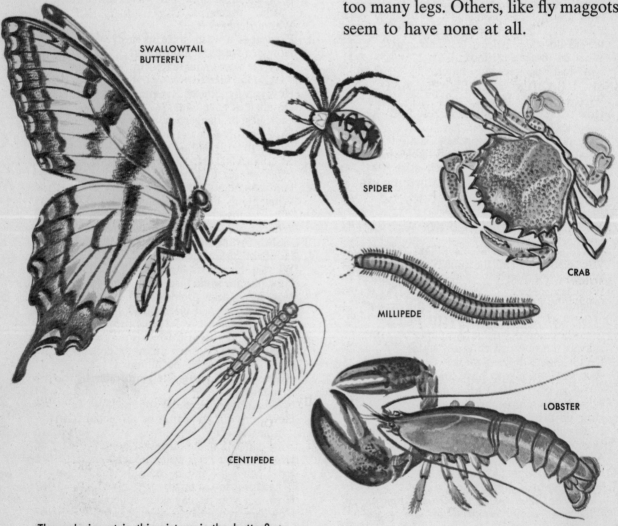

SWALLOWTAIL BUTTERFLY

SPIDER

CRAB

MILLIPEDE

CENTIPEDE

LOBSTER

The only insect in this picture is the butterfly.

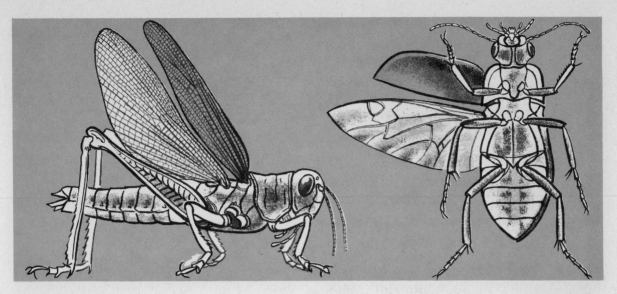

The structure of insects is shown in a side view of a grasshopper and an underside view of a black beetle.

Another way to identify an insect is to count the number of main body parts. Looking at the butterfly, you can see that it has three main body sections:

What are the parts of an insect's body?

(1) A head, with the antennae, or "feelers."

(2) A chest or thorax with all the wings and legs.

(3) A tail-section or abdomen.

The spider seems to have only two parts. Crabs seem to have only one. Scorpions and centipedes have many. And they all have many legs and no wings. So they are not insects.

Why aren't spiders insects?

Not all insects have wings, either. Fleas, some crickets, and even some beetles and moths cannot fly at all. But they still have the right number of legs and body parts as insects—six legs and three main body sections. In fact, the name *insect* comes from a word which means "in sections."

Nobody knows exactly how many kinds of insects there are, but we are sure that there must be more than a million different kinds. Some scientists think there may be seven or eight million kinds — perhaps even more. But we do know that there are more kinds of insects crawling and swimming and flying around than all the other kinds of animals put together.

How many kinds of insects are there?

Each of these insects has its own interesting story. One kind of wasp makes jugs of mud which bake so hard in the sun that they look like stones. Some ants raise plants in tiny gardens. One fly catches a mosquito and lays its eggs on it. Then when the mosquito bites a person, the fly-maggots drop off and burrow under the person's skin.

How are insects different from each other?

There are insects which look like sticks. One of them, the giant walking stick, may be more than a foot long and wider than your finger. It is brown and scaly-looking, like a branch. Its six legs and two antennae look like twigs.

Some insects look like plant parts.

How can some insects hide in plain sight? Have you ever chased a bright orange butterfly in the woods? Its colors may be seen many yards away. Just when you think you have it, it disappears. No matter how hard you look, you can't find it. Then it suddenly flies up from right under your feet. If you catch it, then you know why it has been so hard to see. Its bright wings are the color of a dead leaf on the underside. When it folds its wings, the underside is all that shows. It looks like an old brown leaf.

17-year cicada nymphs. Cicadas include 75 species.

The dead-leaf butterfly looks like the leaves near it.

Many moths can hide in plain sight on the trunk of a tree. Their speckled color is just like that of the bark. A long-legged water bug looks like a floating wisp of hay. Some green insects are shaped just like leaves, while others look like flowers.

One of the most interesting stories is that of the 17-year cicada. It lives seventeen years in darkness below the earth as a nymph. Then suddenly, millions of them come out at once. They leave little holes in the ground about the size of a dime. They cluster so heavily on bushes and trees that the branches bend down with what seem to be large dark berries.

Sometimes insects use tools to help them with their work.

How and why do insects use tools? One wasp picks up a pebble and uses it to pack the ground on top of its eggs. A certain ant uses its babies just as you would use a tube of glue. The ant picks up the baby and presses it against the edges of a curled leaf. The sticky material from the baby's mouth glues the leaf edges together. The ant lion sometimes throws pebbles up into the air so that an insect may be knocked down into its pit — and eaten.

Did you ever forget where you left a hammer or shovel? This couldn't happen to many insects which have their tools with them at all times. The mole cricket has big feet which look like shovels. Burrowing beetles have shovels on the end of their snouts. They are just right for digging the soil. Water striders have waterproof boots in the form of big legs and feet which let them run around on top of the water without getting wet. Diving beetles have a little air-pocket. Then they can breathe under water, like a little skindiver.

The praying mantis has spiny legs which open and close like a jackknife, holding its food tightly. A fly walks upside down on the ceiling because of special pads and hooks which hold it in place. The ichneumon fly has a long drill at the end of its body. With this it can drill deep into a tree trunk to lay its egg in the hole of a wood borer. The tiger beetle has stiff hairs on its feet so it can run over the sand of the beach without slipping.

Bees carry many tools. They have combs and brushes on their legs. These help them work with the wax of the hive. They have a basket to carry the pollen from flowers. Wing-hooks keep their front and hind wings hitched together when they fly. These become unhooked when the bee folds its wings.

Where do insects live? You can find insects nearly everywhere you look. Mountain climbers find them on high peaks. Explorers bring up blind white crickets from deep caves. Little gray insects called spring-tails skip about on winter snows. Their dark-colored bodies soak up the warm sunshine and keep them from freezing.

One kind of insect lives right on the edge of Niagara Falls. It is kept from being swept over the falls by a strong thread holding it in place. Other kinds live only in the still water of ponds. Many live inside the stems of weeds. Some fly high into the air, while others spend their lives within a few inches of where they were hatched. If you look at the skin of an orange, you may see some tiny brown scales. These are scale insects, and they don't move at all. Other scales move very little.

Some insects live under rugs and furniture. They may sometimes find their way into your breakfast cereal. Termites and carpenter ants may tunnel through the boards of your house. One little fellow seems to like books. It spends all of its life in libraries.

Why aren't there any insects in the ocean? There is one great place on earth where insects are not found, and that is the ocean. Insects have never been able to do very well in the seas. Their bodies cannot get used to the salt water. Only a few kinds go into the sea at all, and these stay right near shore. So, even though there are millions of insects, they are crowded close together and fenced in by the oceans that surround us.

Tools that cannot be forgotten:

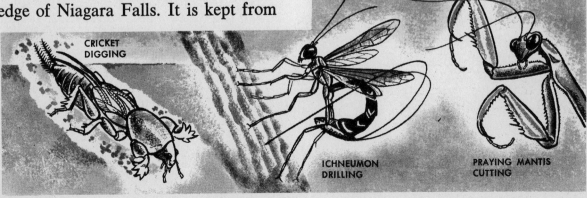

CRICKET DIGGING

ICHNEUMON DRILLING

PRAYING MANTIS CUTTING

Life in a Suit of Armor

If you cut open an insect, you'd never find any bones, no matter how hard you looked. Its skin is the only skeleton an insect has. Without it, the insect would be soft and helpless.

What does an insect look like inside?

Flies and mosquitoes have thin skeletons. The beetle looks like a knight in armor with its thick heavy shell. Even soft aphids live in a thin jacket.

If you wore a space suit that covered your hands and face, how would you be able to feel and smell? You would need little holes to sniff through, and other holes for your fingers to feel through. Insects have tiny hairs which

How are insects able to touch, smell and taste?

Cutaway view of a grasshopper

poke out through the armor. They also have little pits and pockets. These hairs and pockets help them smell and touch and taste.

Sometimes these pockets and hairs are on the legs of the insect. Many of them are on the feelers or antennae.

They may be on other parts of the body. So we can say that some insects "smell" with many parts of their bodies, instead of just through a nose. In fact, insects don't even have noses at all.

Look carefully along the sides of a large insect. Your magnifying glass may show you a row of round circles, looking like the portholes of a ship. These are the breathing pores. They are known as spiracles. Instead of breathing through noses, as we do, insects breathe through holes in their sides.

How do insects breathe?

The spiracles lead to little tubes. These branch all over the inside of the

INSECT SPIRACLE

Bird taking a dust bath

body, even into the legs and eyes. When the insect moves, air is pumped in and out. Even water insects have these tubes. They get their oxygen from the water around them.

Birds take a dust bath to suffocate insect pests in their feathers. The dust clogs up the insects' spiracles, and since they cannot breathe, they die.

When we talk or sing, the noise comes from our throats. A singing insect makes its noise by buzzing or scraping. Crickets rub their wings together. Grasshoppers rub their legs and wings together. Cicadas have a drum on their bodies. Other insects scratch their bodies or grind their jaws to make a noise. They find each other by following these noises. Sometimes they use the noises to frighten away their enemies.

How do insects "talk"?

Katydids have little patches on their legs which are sensitive to noises. Grasshoppers have their ears on their abdomen. Some insects can feel sounds or vibrations through their feet, just as you can feel a radio playing by touching it with your fingers. Scientists have not yet found the ears of the champion noisemaker of them all, the cicada. As far as they have been able to discover, it has no ears. It seems to make all that noise for nothing.

How do insects hear?

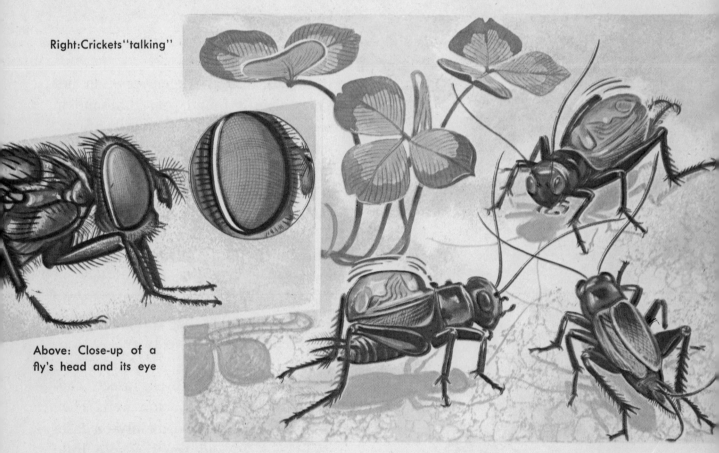

Right: Crickets "talking"

Above: Close-up of a fly's head and its eye

When insects fly, their wings make a humming sound. Sometimes the muscles of the insect make a hum, as well. The higher the hum, the faster the wings are beating. A buzzing housefly beats its wings twenty thousand times a minute.

If you think insects have just two eyes, you have guessed too low. What appear to be two eyes are really many small ones packed together. They are called facets.

There may be more than fifty facets

How many eyes do insects have?

in each of the two large eyes of an ant. One scientist found four thousand in each large eye of a housefly. Some moths and dragonflies may have a total of fifty thousand facets!

For many insects, even this great number does not seem to be enough. They also have a few single eyes right in front of the head. These look like colored beads. They probably help to see things up close, like little magnifying glasses. The big compound eyes help see things farther away.

Even with all these eyes, insects cannot see too well. They depend mainly on taste and smell. Those little hairs and pits on the body and antennae are very keen. Many male moths have big, feathery antennae which help them find the female in the dark. One scientist found that some moths can find another moth as far as a mile away.

How do insects find their way?

Run a finger across an ant trail to confuse the ants.

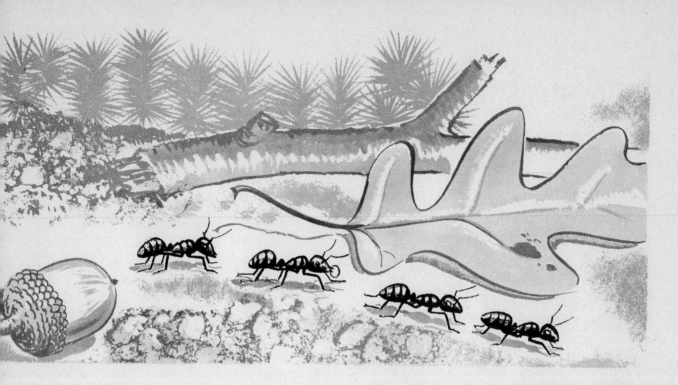

If you have a chance, watch some ants at work. They feel along the ground with their antennae, following definite trails which lead them back to the nest. Each ant follows the trail of the one ahead of it.

Now wipe your finger hard across the trail several times. This will brush away much of the scent. Then watch the next ant that comes along. It stops, turns circles, goes from side to side. It seems completely lost, even if the nest is only a few inches away. It may take three or four minutes for it to find its way again.

One scientist saw a long line of caterpillars. Each was following the one ahead of it. The line went over logs and under bushes, like a little train.

Then he had an idea. He put some of them on the edge of a glass bowl. Around and around they went, following each other's trail in a circle for days and days. They never stopped or climbed down. They just kept on playing follow-the-leader until the scientist took them off.

This was more than just a game for the scientist. He was finding out some important things about insects. Other scientists were also studying them.

Scientists found that insects know how **How do insects know what to do?** to act as soon as they are born. We have to learn to nail boards together, but insects can make perfect homes on the first try. Our parents help us decide what food to eat, but insects usually never see their parents. The hungry babies know what to eat as soon as they hatch. They know how to hide their eggs, and keep out of danger.

They can do these things because of what we call "instinct." This usually helps the insect meet all its problems. Instinct tells a Japanese beetle to drop to the ground out of sight the minute you touch its twig. Instinct tells a

11

bombardier beetle to wave its abdomen in the air and squirt you with a bad-smelling spray, like a little skunk. Instinct helps a squash bug put its eggs where they will be hidden, and yet near the best food.

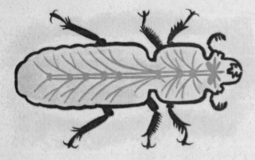

Ganglia (nerve centers) make up an insect's nervous system. They run lengthwise and a double chain of nerves connects them. Nerves branch from each *ganglion* to other parts of the body. The large pair of ganglia in the front is called the "brain."

Instinct is some kind of inner knowledge that helps the insect to do something, although the insect has never been shown how to do it. So instinct may be described as built-in or ready-made knowledge. Scientists, however, don't know what causes it, or how it was made.

Although many insects eat our gardens and forests, some kinds are useful to us. Perhaps you have

How do insects help us?

watched a pair of burying beetles as they dug under a dead mouse until it sank into the ground out of sight. Maybe you have seen ants cleaning up some garbage by taking it into their nest. One kind even carries away cigarette butts.

Ladybird beetles eat plant lice. Some kinds of stinkbugs feed on harmful caterpillars. Water striders keep the water clean by feeding on insects which drop from the bushes. Hornets fly around cows and horses, chasing the flies until they catch one for food.

Perhaps you have seen a painter using shellac. It looks like varnish and is used on boats and airplanes. It comes from the lac insect of India. Some brightly-colored dyes are also made from insects. Silk is made by silkworms to cover their cocoons. The Chinese keep singing crickets in little cages. Even the ground-up bodies of some insects are made into medicine.

Carefully taste a drop of liquid found in the bottom of a flower.

Why do the bees visit the flowers?

It is used by the bees in making honey. When the beekeeper takes the honeycomb from the hive, he always leaves plenty for the bees to eat during the winter. Otherwise they would starve.

When bees go from one flower to another for the sweet nectar they make into food, they also pick up some pollen on the hairs of their body and legs. A

little of this pollen brushes off as they visit each new flower. It helps the flowers' seeds and fruit to grow. Without bees, plants couldn't produce apples, peaches, melons and other good things we have to eat.

Fireflies in a cage make a useful "insect lantern" for the natives of some tropical lands.

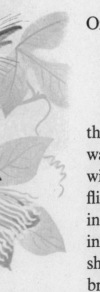

One of the strangest uses for insects is that of lighting a room. In many parts of the world there are no electric lights. When the natives in some tropical countries want to see after dark, they go outdoors with a little cage. They put a few fireflies in the cage. Each firefly has a spot in its body which glows when air is let in through the insect's air tubes. The shining of a dozen large fireflies helps brighten up the room. Some native girls even wear a firefly in their hair.

Where are insects used for lanterns?

Fresh Eggs—Handle With Care

INSECTS have many enemies and it is not surprising that they have found many ways to protect themselves. Each one has its own special way of caring for itself.

Even the eggs are given special care by the mother insect. **How are the eggs protected?** How often do you see any insect eggs? If you were able to count all the eggs within a few miles of your house this minute, you would find that there were millions of them. Yet you might look for a long time before you could find any at all.

Some insect mothers bury their eggs deep in the soil. Grasshoppers poke the end of their bodies down as far as they can reach, and lay their eggs in the hole. Some beetles dig down out of sight to lay their eggs. Ants and termites have nests under a stump or in a mound of earth. There the eggs are safely hidden and protected from enemies. Some insects produce a liquid into which they put their eggs. Later, the liquid hardens and the eggs are safe in a covering.

Sometimes you can find insect eggs on leaves and twigs. They **Where can insect eggs be found?** may have tough shells so that other insects cannot eat them. They

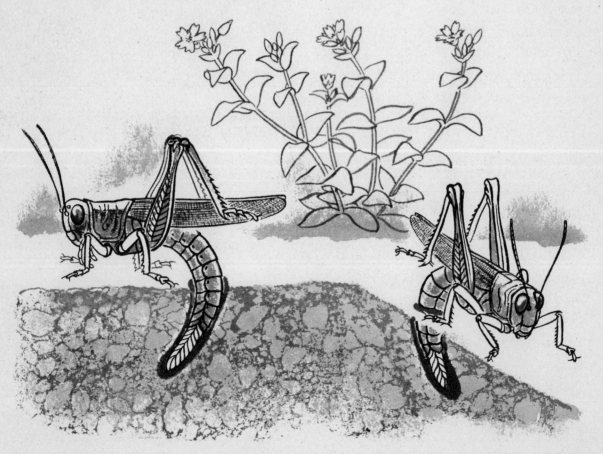

Grasshoppers poke their abdomens into the earth as far down as they can reach to lay from 20 to 100 eggs.

may be covered with wax to protect them from winter winds. Perhaps you have seen the egg case of a praying mantis. This fluffy case is like a blanket in the snow. The eggs are safe inside.

You may find a green twig which looks as if someone had been cutting it with a knife. Possibly you will find an insect egg at the bottom of each cut. A cicada makes the cuts with the sharp tip of its body. Then the eggs are safely hidden under the bark.

There are many other places where you can find the eggs of insects. Flies lay their eggs in garbage. Lice attach their eggs to the hair of animals with a special glue of their own. Some walking-stick insects drop thousands of eggs from the trees. It sounds like falling rain. Clothes moths lay tiny eggs in the wrinkles of coats and suits and other cloth garments.

Where do water insects lay their eggs?

Mosquitoes lay large numbers of eggs on the water. Examine the underside of a water lily leaf. You'll find many kinds of eggs. Perhaps you have seen a dragonfly darting along over a pond. It dips down every few seconds to drop an egg beneath the water.

Some damselflies hitch together like a little train. Then the mother fly goes beneath the surface of the water to lay her eggs, while the father fly stays above. When the eggs are laid, the male pulls the female out of the water.

Here is a "damsel train" in action. The female damselfly lays her eggs in the water or else on water plants.

15

TAILED BLUE BUTTERFLY

AMERICAN COPPER BUTTERFLY

ATTEVA AUREA MOTH

ANGLEWING BUTTERFLY

SWALLOWTAIL BUTTERFLY

ROADSIDE BUTTERFLY

ZEBRA SWALLOWTAIL BUTTERFLY

HAIRSTREAK BUTTERFLY

BUCKEYE BUTTERFLY

ACHEMON SPHINX MOTH

FRITILLARY BUTTERFLY

STRIPED MORNING SPHINX MOTH

BELLA MOTH

GRACEFUL CLEARWING MOTH

ORANGE SULPHUR BUTTERFLY

APANTESIS MOTH

One female water bug makes the male bug take care of the eggs. She catches him and lays her eggs on his back!

What do insect eggs look like? Some of these eggs are round. Others are flat. Some are brightly colored. Others are wrinkled and brown. Many are black. There are eggs shaped like the crown of a king. Others look like little jugs with pop-up lids. If you have a magnifying glass, you can see various shapes and sizes of insect eggs.

How fast do insect eggs hatch? Some tent caterpillar eggs take two years to hatch. Fly eggs may hatch in a few hours. Many eggs laid in the fall will not hatch until spring. Some eggs hatch inside the mother insect, so that tiny insect babies are born.

MONARCH EGG ENLARGED

This monarch butterfly hides her eggs under a leaf.

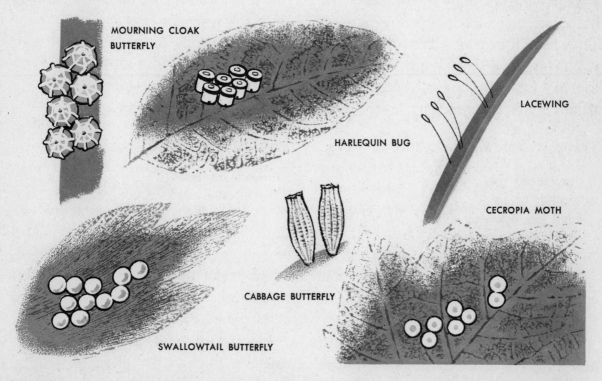

MOURNING CLOAK BUTTERFLY

HARLEQUIN BUG

LACEWING

CECROPIA MOTH

CABBAGE BUTTERFLY

SWALLOWTAIL BUTTERFLY

Insects lay eggs of various shapes, sizes and colors. All the insect eggs pictured here have been enlarged.

17

A cicada killer buries its victim in an underground passage. The paralyzed cicada has been stung and will provide food for the larva of the cicada killer when the egg hatches later on.

Insect Babies—All Shapes and Sizes

Moths and butterflies lay eggs which hatch out into caterpillars. Big, buzzing bumblebees have little grubs for babies. So do beetles and wasps. Fly eggs hatch into maggots. Caterpillars, grubs and maggots are called larvae.

What are insect babies like?

Grasshoppers and dragonflies have babies which look a lot like the parents. They have little buds where their wings will grow some day. Their heads seem too big for their bodies. These insect babies are called nymphs.

There is one way in which all these different babies are alike. They are nearly always hungry. They begin to eat soon after they hatch, and keep on eating for most of their lives. So the eggs are laid where the insects will have food as soon as they hatch.

How does the mother insect feed her babies?

Perhaps you have seen a wasp pulling and tugging at a caterpillar that had been stung so that it couldn't move. The wasp will poke it down into a new hole in the soil where she has laid her eggs. The new wasp babies will then have food to eat when they hatch.

Some new insect babies are so hungry that they will eat anything at all — even their own brothers and sisters. But the lacewing fly has solved this problem. She lays each egg at the end of a long stalk. When the fierce little baby hatches, it drops off the stalk and begins to hunt for food. Its brothers and sisters are safe on their stalks above.

New baby insects can protect themselves, even in a world filled with hungry enemies. Many of them are the same color as the leaves they eat, so that they are hard to see. Some have fierce-looking spots which make them seem to have great round eyes. Some have sharp spines, making them look like tiny cactus plants.

How do baby insects protect themselves?

One insect puts out a pair of bad-smelling horns when it is in danger. Some insects are long and brown and look just like a twig. Others are round and gray like a pebble. Sharp-jawed ones may pinch you if you bother them. Others curl up and drop into the grass at the slightest touch. Still others are poisonous. Their enemies soon learn not to eat them. Baby insects find protection in their shapes, colors, odors, body poisons and fierce looks.

Most insect babies have no parents to take care of them. The adult insects, their mothers and fathers, usually die

What kind of homes do insect babies have?

soon after the eggs are laid. Wasps, bees, ants and termites, however, take good care of their children. They build nests with many caves and tunnels. Here they have rooms that may be compared to our nurseries, kitchens and storehouses. These nests may be many feet high, and some are twice as tall as a man.

Many baby insects build homes of their own. The caddisfly larva lives on the bottom of streams and ponds. It

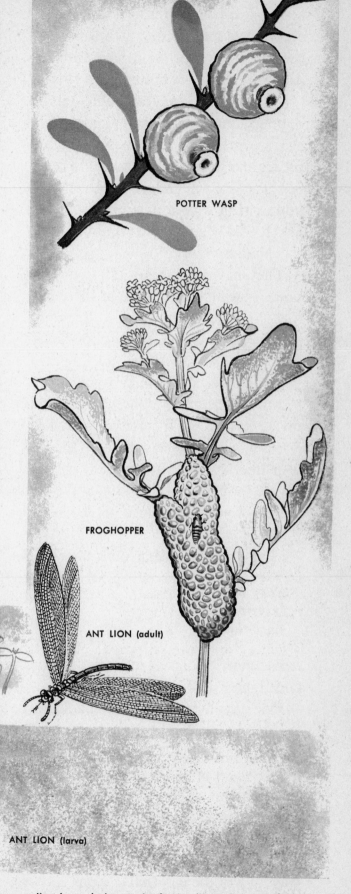

POTTER WASP

FROGHOPPER

ANT LION (adult)

ANT LION (larva)

Insects build nests of many shapes and materials. The ant lion larva below waits for its dinner in a sand pit.

makes a tube of sticks or sand grains glued together. Then it fits itself inside the tube. It looks like a little turtle as it bumps along the bottom of a stream.

One of the strangest homes is the bubble house of the froghopper. You can see many of these nests on grass blades and weeds. If you poke inside the bubbles, you will find a little green froghopper. Put it on a new blade of grass and it will begin to blow bubbles until it is hidden.

The ant lion makes a pit in the dry sand. It waits at the bottom of the pit with its pincers open wide. If an ant stumbles into the pit, the ant lion has its dinner.

Some caterpillars make webs to protect themselves. Other insect babies roll up leaves or cover themselves with dust. Some tiny insects even tunnel in the leaf of a tree, leaving strange marks. Once people thought that the trails of the leaf miners were the writings of ghosts.

The baby insects keep on eating and growing. But they **Why do baby insects split their skins?** don't grow just as we do. An insect's skin doesn't stretch to make more room. It becomes tighter and tighter, like last year's jacket.

One day it splits along the back, and the young insect crawls out of its old skin. Its new skin is soft and thin, and its body swells up quickly. Soon the new skin hardens. Then the insect can no longer grow until after it splits its jacket again.

Only young insects can grow in this way. When the caterpillar turns into a moth, or the grub becomes a beetle, they will never shed their skin again. They stay the same size for the rest of their lives. Little moths don't become big moths, nor little flies big ones.

Some insects are so noisy when they **Does an insect make sounds when it eats?** eat that you can hear them. Perhaps you have heard a scratching sound coming from a wood pile in the forest. It may have been a family of wood borers, a kind of beetle grub. You can often hear them chewing away.

Maybe you have read, in the Bible, about locusts that attacked crops in ancient times, or in the newspapers, about locust attacks in more recent years. Millions of locusts eating a field of grain can be heard some distance away. They sound like the wind in dry leaves.

A cricket or beetle grub chews its food. But some insects sip their food quietly through a long tube. They drink the sap of plants or the blood of animals. If you look where their mouth should be, all you see is a long, pointed tube. Think how it must be to go around with your mouth shut tight and just a straw sticking out!

Who eats more food — you or your **How much does an insect eat?** parents? Many growing insects eat much more than their mother and father eat together. They may eat more than their own weight in food each day. They are growing so fast that they never seem to get enough food.

20

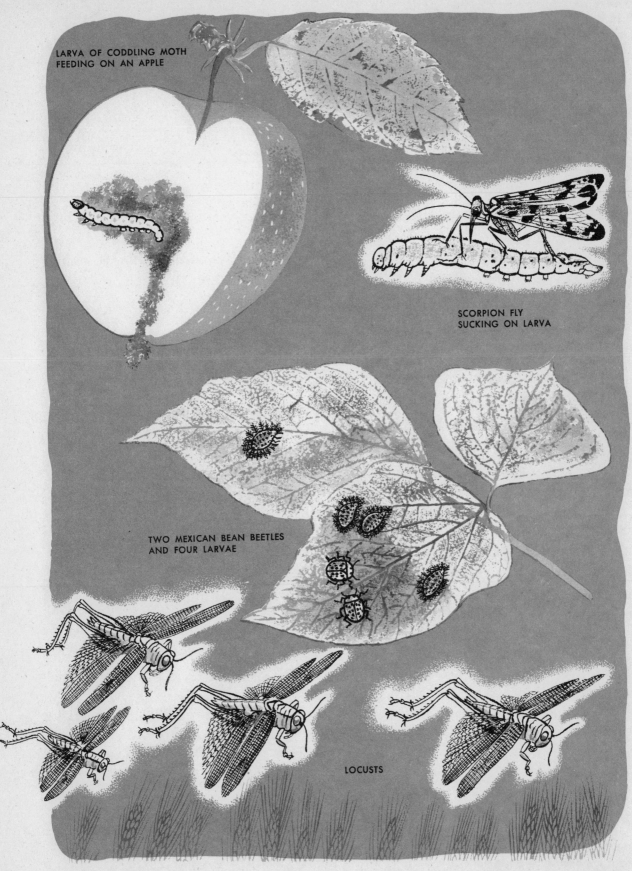

LARVA OF CODDLING MOTH
FEEDING ON AN APPLE

SCORPION FLY
SUCKING ON LARVA

TWO MEXICAN BEAN BEETLES
AND FOUR LARVAE

LOCUSTS

Insects are big eaters. Not only do they feed upon plants, fruit and other insects, but they also feed on woolens, leather, fur, furniture and even books. Locusts are great crop destroyers. Fortunately, birds feed upon them.

A spice-bush swallowtail caterpillar

The Unlucky Caterpillar

HAVE you ever watched a caterpillar on the sidewalk? Maybe you've seen it chewing on some leaves. If you have a garden, perhaps you have helped spray the plants so it wouldn't eat them.

When the caterpillar eats leaves that have been sprayed with a poisonous chemical, the poison may kill it. At least, the poisonous chemical will cause it to move away.

The caterpillar has been in danger ever **What are the** since its butterfly-**caterpillar's** mother first laid her **enemies?** eggs. No matter how carefully the eggs are hidden, other insects come along looking for tiny bits of food, and often find them. Storms and cold weather kill many caterpillars in the eggs, too.

When the egg hatches, insects and spiders are waiting for the caterpillar's

Birds are one of the caterpillar's main enemies and help to control many kinds of insect pests.

CECROPIA MOTH (adult)

COCOON

LARVA SPINNING COCOON

LARVA MOLTING

Illustrated here is the life cycle of a cecropia moth.

appearance. Birds look at every leaf and twig, eating every caterpillar they can find. Snakes, lizards, toads and frogs catch more of them. And when you go out in the field to make an insect collection, you will catch some, too.

Look at the head of the next caterpillar you find. It seems **Can it see its enemies?** to have two great round eyes in front, but they're not eyes at all. The real eyes are little pinpoint dots which can hardly be seen. It can see only a few inches ahead. Probably the only way the caterpillar

LARVAE EATING

LARVAE GROWING LARGER

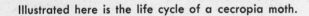
GGS

LARVAE HATCHED FROM EGGS

knows danger is near is when the leaf shakes as a bird lands near it, or when it smells the scent of a nearby enemy.

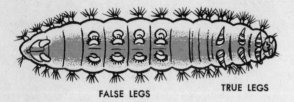

FALSE LEGS   TRUE LEGS

This bottom view of a caterpillar shows its true and false legs. The temporary prolegs will be shed later.

How many legs has a caterpillar? A caterpillar's body is divided into thirteen ringlike parts (segments). Attached to the three segments nearest the head, in the thorax body section, the caterpillar has six little, stubby legs. It also has a few extra pairs of legs along the sides of the segments which make up the abdomen body section. These false legs, called prolegs, are temporary and the caterpillar will shed them along with the last skin.

Why does it eat all the time? You may like a snack after school, or just before going to bed, but the caterpillar is always hungry, and eats almost all day and all night. It needs a great deal of food because it is growing so fast. So it keeps munching on the turnips and radishes in the garden. If the caterpillar has to go without food for more than a few hours it will starve.

What is "molting"? As a caterpillar eats, it continues to grow. However, like other insects, the caterpillar's skin doesn't grow as the rest of its body does. It remains the same size so that, finally, the tight skin splits. The caterpillar then sheds its skin by wriggling out, a process that is called "molting." But underneath is another skin. The caterpillar will outgrow this one, too. In fact, it will molt several times until it reaches the end of the caterpillar stage, and is fully grown.

What is a pupa? After it molts for the last time, the caterpillar becomes a pupa. This is the stage when it goes down into a hole in the earth, or attaches itself to a leaf on a tree. Sometimes it spins silk

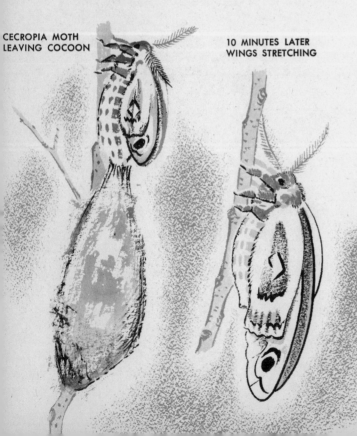

CECROPIA MOTH LEAVING COCOON

10 MINUTES LATER WINGS STRETCHING

20 MINUTES LATER WINGS FULLY STRETCHED

threads about itself until it looks like a bit of fluff. This is called a cocoon, the name most people use when they refer to the pupal stage. Maybe you can find a pupa if you look under old boards, leaves or stones.

You'd think it would be safe in the hard pupal shell. But mice nip at pupas with their sharp teeth. Skunks and raccoons dig them up. Even big, shuffling bears tear old stumps and logs apart until they find them.

Finally the great day comes when the pupal stage is over. For

What does it look like when it is full-grown? some insects, it is only a few weeks, but for most insects, the pupal stage usually lasts the whole winter. Then, in the spring, the pupal shell cracks open and out crawls the insect. It is no longer a caterpillar, however. Now it is a moth, or a butterfly with shining wings. The butterfly spreads its wings to dry in the sunshine. Then it flies away, leaving the pupal shell behind.

If larvae have so many troubles, how can there be so many butterflies and bees and other insects in this world? The answer is one of Nature's most wonderful stories.

Insects develop in any one of three different ways. At the top is the life cycle of a silverfish. This insect looks like its parents as soon as it hatches from the egg and grows gradually until it reaches adult size. This is called gradual development. In the center is the life cycle of the dragonfly which has an incomplete metamorphosis or development. *Metamorphosis* means "change of form." The butterfly shown below has a complete metamorphosis. Its life cycle includes four stages — the egg, larva, pupa and adult stage.

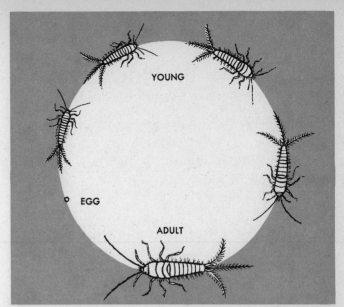

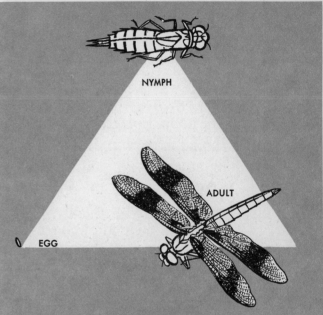

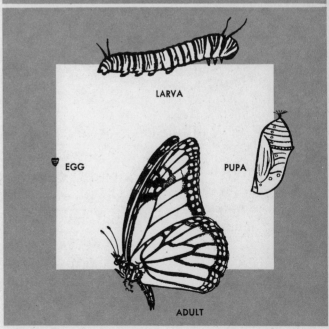

House of Mystery—the Pupa

What is going on inside the pupa? If you find a pupa or silk-wrapped cocoon, look at it carefully. It's hard to know just what it will be when it hatches out. But if your eyes are sharp, you'll see wrinkles and folds where the new wings will be. You can find the eyes, the mouth and the legs. But unless you see it twist or turn, it seems more dead than alive.

Inside the pupa, there's a wonderful change taking place. Instead of stubby little baby legs, there are the strong new legs of the adult. Folded wings are waiting to spread in the sun. Big round eyes and long antennae are getting ready to help it find its way in the world. The head, mouth and body are all different. No matter how hard you looked inside a pupa, you couldn't find the caterpillar or grub any more.

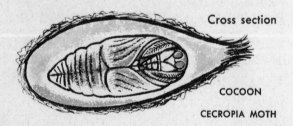

Cross section

COCOON
CECROPIA MOTH

Why is the pupa so carefully hidden? Think of all the changes you'd have to make in order to turn into a bird. You'd have to grow feathers, a beak, wings and claws. All the time you were changing, you'd be wrapped up so tight you couldn't move. This is about what an insect has to do as it changes from a pupa to an adult. No wonder it is hidden deep under a log or curled up in a leaf, where it's safe!

SILKWORM COCOON

Do all insects have a pupa? Do all insects go through this great change? Most of them do, but not those which hatch out of their eggs looking like their parents. Praying mantis nymphs change slowly until they become adults. So do cockroach and squash bug nymphs. Each time they split their skin and grow a new one, they look more like the adult, so they do not need any pupal stage.

SWALLOWTAIL BUTTERFLY PUPA

Why do some pupas have an anchor? Some insects anchor the pupa in place with a strong thread. Then, when they pull themselves out later, the old brown shell will stay in place. Other insects seem to do as well without an anchor. Some black flies anchor the pupa under water. They also have a little bubble. When they break out of the pupal case, they ride to the surface in the bubble. When the bubble bursts they fly away.

Mourning cloak larva (left) changing to pupal stage.

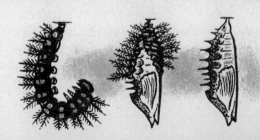

Jack Frost Arrives

The temperature of an insect changes **What is the temperature of an insect?** according to the weather in the insect's surroundings, so that its temperature is always changing.

In the winter, the insects hidden in the ground and under the bark of trees are just about as cold as the snow. They are so cold that they can hardly move at all. In the summer, they are nearly as hot as the sunshine. Then they run and fly very quickly.

If you listen to a cricket chirping, you can guess the temperature outdoors. The warmer the day, the faster the song. One kind, the snowy tree cricket, sings the same musical note over and over. Count the number of times it sings in fifteen seconds. Then add forty. The resulting number will approximate the reading on a thermometer.

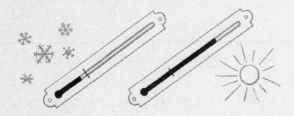

You might think that because insects get so cold in **How do insects spend the winter?** winter, you would want to bring them all in by the fire where it is warm. But if they were kept alive and active in a warm house they would starve to death without any food. So it is better that they spend the winter months outdoors. There they just remain quiet until spring comes again.

Sometimes they come out on a warm day. Then you see flies buzzing around the sunny side of a house. Sometimes you see caterpillars crawling slowly on the bark of trees. The mourning cloak butterfly often comes out on a sunny January day. It looks quite out of place sailing over the patches of snow.

Insects may spend the winter as a pupa or larva. Other insects lay their eggs during late summer and then die. The only thing that keeps them from dying out completely is the cluster of eggs. Like tiny seeds, they wait for spring. Then, sure enough, they hatch out. They grow up to be just like the parents they never saw.

A few insects are active all year, even **How can some insects keep warm in the winter?** where the winters are cold. Lice and fleas which live on birds and animals keep warm in the thick fur and feathers. Cave insects crawl around as usual, for the temperature hardly changes at all inside a cave.

Even on a winter day when the temperature is far below zero, and snow and ice are everywhere, bees are active in their hives. If you should visit an apiary

The fur of a monkey is a warm hiding place for insects.

27

(a place where bees are kept) on a winter day, put your ear against a beehive and listen. You will hear a faint humming sound. Inside the hive, even on a cold day, bees move around slowly, buzzing their wings. This activity keeps them warm enough so that they won't freeze.

A warm beehive sometimes attracts mice and other animals. If a mouse finds the hive, it may eat some of the honey the bees have stored for food. It may build its nest in front of the entrance so that the bees cannot get out in the spring.

Often the bees drive the mouse away with their stings. Sometimes they sting it so much that it dies. Then they have to leave the body there. But the bees often cover a dead mouse with their wax, sealing it up so that the air in the hive will stay fresh.

Are there any insect travelers? A few insects go south in the winter, just as the birds do. The big orange-and-black monarch butterfly may travel from Canada to Mexico. It goes in flocks of thousands. Sometimes it crosses many miles of water over the Great Lakes and the Gulf of Mexico. Nobody yet knows how it finds its way. It is one of the greatest of all insect travelers.

The mouse has a sweet tooth, especially for honey, but bees know how to defend their property from enemies.

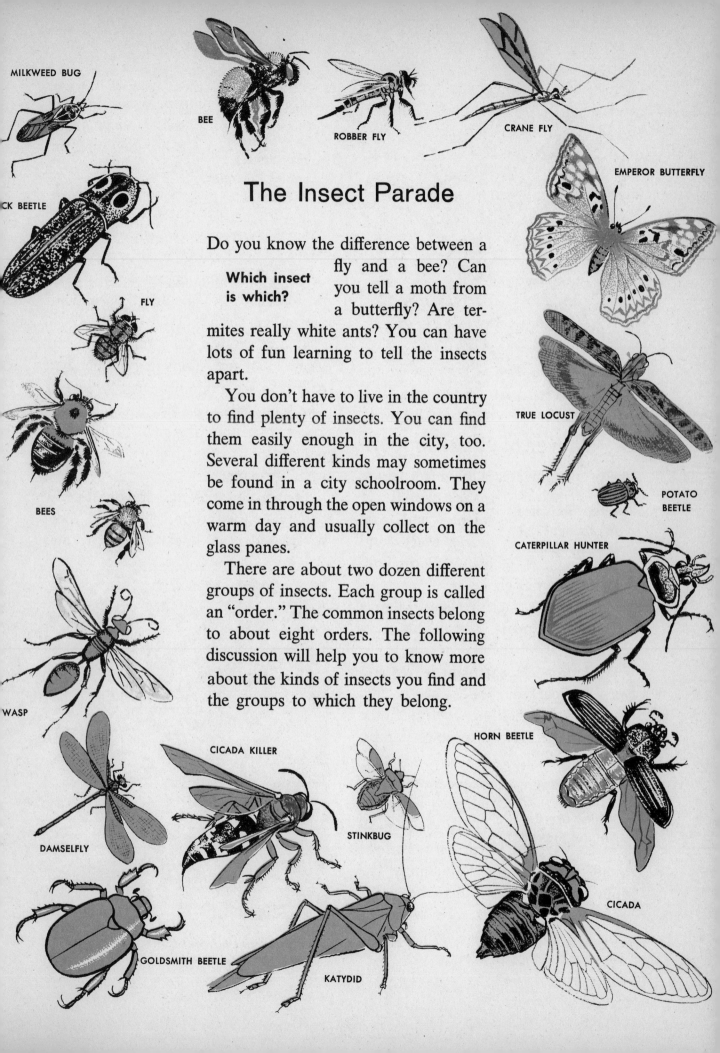

MILKWEED BUG

BEE

ROBBER FLY

CRANE FLY

EMPEROR BUTTERFLY

CK BEETLE

FLY

BEES

TRUE LOCUST

POTATO BEETLE

CATERPILLAR HUNTER

WASP

HORN BEETLE

DAMSELFLY

CICADA KILLER

STINKBUG

CICADA

GOLDSMITH BEETLE

KATYDID

The Insect Parade

Do you know the difference between a fly and a bee? Can you tell a moth from a butterfly? Are termites really white ants? You can have lots of fun learning to tell the insects apart.

Which insect is which?

You don't have to live in the country to find plenty of insects. You can find them easily enough in the city, too. Several different kinds may sometimes be found in a city schoolroom. They come in through the open windows on a warm day and usually collect on the glass panes.

There are about two dozen different groups of insects. Each group is called an "order." The common insects belong to about eight orders. The following discussion will help you to know more about the kinds of insects you find and the groups to which they belong.

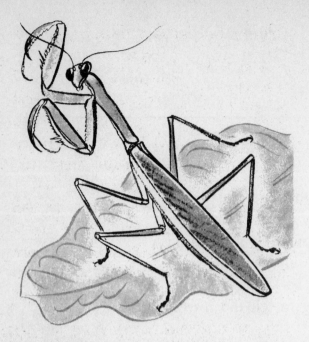

A praying mantis sits upon a leaf that it will soon eat.

1. Relatives of Grasshoppers

The praying mantis is the terror of the

What are some relatives of the grasshoppers?

insect world. It catches and eats nearly every kind of insect it can find.

It belongs in this group.

The walking stick is also a relative of the grasshoppers. So are the cockroaches.

Walking sticks eat plant leaves and twigs, but cockroaches eat nearly anything. Cockroaches have even eaten the glue from the backs of postage stamps.

Crickets and grasshoppers are the most

Which are the "music makers"?

musical of insects. They make most of the insect

sounds you hear in the country. The mole cricket even sings under the ground. Locusts buzz their wings together as they fly, and katydids call from the treetops at night.

2. The Dragonflies

Walk near a swamp or brook in sum-

Why were dragonflies called "darning needles"?

mer, and you may see many dragonflies. People used to think they would sew up your ears

while you were asleep. They called them "darning needles." Of course, they don't do any such thing. They are really helpful insects, for they catch thousands of mosquitoes.

If you catch a dragonfly, notice its large eyes and funny legs. The eyes help it to see in almost every direction. The legs form a basket to catch other insects as it flies along. With its wings pointed out to the side, it looks like a small airplane.

Damselflies look like dragonflies and belong to this group. They fold their wings and point them up in the air.

Pictured above is a termite family in its nest. At the top left is the male, underneath is the queen and at

30

The nymphs of some dragonflies can travel by jet propulsion. They squirt water out of the end of their bodies. This makes them shoot forward like a little jet airplane. Perhaps it's more like a submarine, though, for they live under the water.

How are young dragonflies jet-propelled?

3. The Termites

If you live in Canada or the northern United States, you may not have seen many termites. They are much more common farther south.

How do termites differ from ants?

Sometimes termites are called "white ants," but they are really not ants at all. Ants have a thin waist between the thorax and abdomen. Termites are thick-bodied from head to tail.

Soldier termites guard the nest from enemies with their powerful jaws. Hundreds of workers build the nest and get the food. The queen lays great numbers of eggs. Sometimes there may be more than one queen, and a few kings as well.

What is a termite family like?

Sometimes you see termites by the thousands as they come out on a window sill or old stump. These are dark-colored kings and queens ready to leave the nest. They fly to a new spot

her side, a soldier, then the king and workers. At the far right are the mounds of some tropical termites.

and then do a strange thing. They break off their wings so they can never fly again. Then they burrow into the ground and start a new colony.

Termites eat nearly everything made

What do termites eat?

out of wood, leaving only a thin outer layer. Once a teacher opened an old desk drawer. Termites had drilled up through the floor and into the desk leg. They had hollowed out the wood of the desk until it was just a shell. When he pulled on the drawer, the desk toppled.

4. The True Bugs

Not all insects are bugs. The only real

Is every insect a bug?

bugs are those with the soda-straw mouths made for poking into plants or drinking the blood of animals. Bugs have four wings or no wings at all. Half of the wing is tough, like a

beetle's. The other half is thin, like that of a fly.

Squash bugs, bedbugs and stinkbugs are all true bugs. So is the diving water boatman with its long legs, which look like oars. Ladybugs and June bugs are not really bugs at all. They are beetles with chewing mouths.

The noisy cicada is a relative of the bugs. So are the green aphids.

Aphids are interesting because they give

Why do ants keep "cows"?

off sweet honeydew which ants love. Some ants even carry aphids down into the ground to feed on the roots of plants. Then they

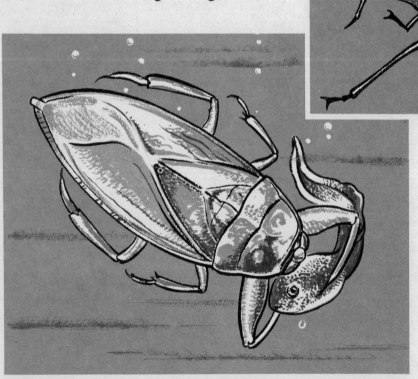

A giant water bug makes a meal of a tadpole. The insert shows a close-up view of a water bug's head and mouth.

have a honeydew supply right in the nest. This is almost like a farmer who keeps cows for milk. So we may say that ants keep aphids as "cows."

Cornfield ants "milking" aphids

5. The Beetles

There are more kinds of beetles than

How many kinds of beetles are known?

any other insect group in the world. If you began collecting beetles at the rate of one new kind every day, your life wouldn't be long enough to collect all of them. It would take seven hundred years. There are more than 250,000 known kinds.

Sprinkle some salt in your hand.

There are beetles so small that they could hide beneath a single grain of salt! There are beetles so large that when they spread their legs they would cover half this page!

Perhaps you remember the Bible story of

Which is one of the largest beetles?

David and Goliath. One of the largest of all insects is the Goliath beetle. It has a body almost as long as a banana. In fact, when a living specimen was sent to a museum, scientists found that it

(Above): Close-up of the head of a male stag beetle.

(Right): Stag beetles, male (top) and female (bottom).

liked to eat bananas. It was found in Africa, and was quite lucky to stay alive long enough to reach America. Some natives in Africa like to fry the giant grubs in oil for food.

You can usually identify a beetle easily when you see it.

How can you tell a beetle from other insects?

It has powerful jaws for chewing. Heavy wings look like two shields on its back. Underneath are the folded wings which are used in flying. The wings of the Goliath beetle may spread eight inches.

Stag beetles have jaws so large they look like the antlers of a tiny deer. Ground beetles have powerful jaws for eating other insects. The jaws of the boll weevil are out at the end of a long snout. It looks like a true bug at first, but if you look close you'll see its jaws.

6. The Moths and Butterflies

Rub your finger gently on the wing of a butterfly or moth. You will find that a soft powder

Why are moths and butterflies called "scale-wings"?

comes off. A microscope would show you that this powder is really thousands of tiny scales. They are arranged on the wing like shingles on a roof.

Some moths are not much larger than a pinhead. The largest may have a wingspan of more than a foot. Some are the most colorful of all insects. They

How large are moths?

may shine bright blue in one light, green or purple in another.

These insects have a coiled tube for sipping liquids instead of the pointed beak of the bugs or the jaws of the

How do moths eat?

beetles. They poke this tube down into flowers to get the sweet nectar.

One time several butterflies, near a group of soldiers standing at attention, flew from one soldier to another. They alighted on each bright-colored shoulder patch and uncoiled their long tubes. The soldiers must have looked like some new flower to the butterflies.

Some moths are helpful to man. We unwind the silk from the silkworm's cocoon. Many caterpillars eat troublesome weeds. But

Are moths helpful to man?

many butterflies and moths have babies which are not so helpful. They eat our gardens, our clothes and our forests. Gypsy moth caterpillars may eat the leaves from hundreds of trees at once.

Look at the way a moth holds its wings. The wings lie down flat over the moth's sides and back. A butterfly

How can you tell a moth from a butterfly?

holds them pointed up over its back. Moths have antennae which look like feathers. The antennae of a butterfly look like long threads with a knot at the end. And, of course, you usually see moths at night and butterflies during the day.

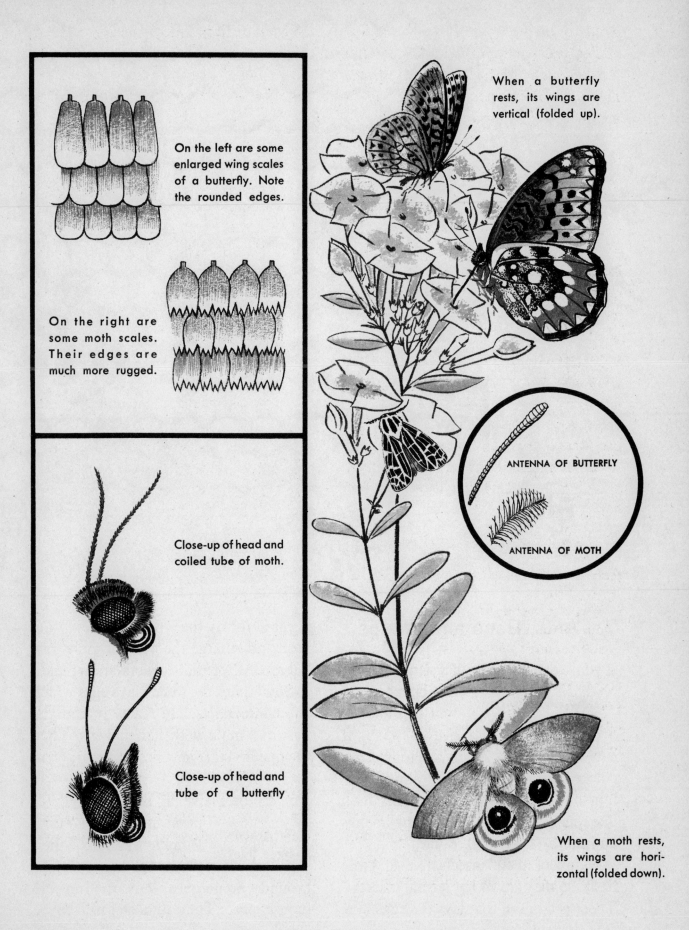

On the left are some enlarged wing scales of a butterfly. Note the rounded edges.

On the right are some moth scales. Their edges are much more rugged.

Close-up of head and coiled tube of moth.

Close-up of head and tube of a butterfly

When a butterfly rests, its wings are vertical (folded up).

ANTENNA OF BUTTERFLY

ANTENNA OF MOTH

When a moth rests, its wings are horizontal (folded down).

7. Ants, Bees and Wasps

If you see an insect with a slender waist,

How do ants, bees and wasps differ from other insects? the chances are that it is an ant, bee or wasp. If it has four clear-colored wings, you can be almost certain of it. Some flies and moths look like them, but flies have only two wings and moths have thick bodies.

Many of these insects live in large nests, so they are called "social insects." There is a queen that lays the eggs. She is cared for by the workers. They bring food and enlarge the nest for more new babies. All of the workers are females.

Sometimes the queen lays eggs which hatch into males. The males fly from the nest and mate with new queens. Then the queens start new nests of their own.

Not all bees live in hives. Carpenter

Where do bees live? bees dig holes in wood. Bumblebees make their home in holes in the ground. Sometimes they use an old mouse nest. They almost seem to be

QUEEN

WORKER

DRONE

A Honeybee Hive

The yellow cells are filled with pollen, the dark cells are ripe with honey, and the tan cells have young bees inside them.

paying the mice back for living in the hives of honeybees.

Mason bees lay their eggs in an old snail shell or knothole. A mason bee might even use a keyhole in a door for its home, cementing it shut with sand and clay.

Wasps and hornets were the first paper

How does a wasp make its nest?

makers. Long before humans learned to grind wood into paper, these insects were chewing bits of sticks, which they then

Paper wasps and their nest

37

mixed with saliva from their mouths. They shaped this material into nests. When it dried, they had a strong paper house in which to live.

Some wasps hunt and kill spiders.

How are wasps helpful to us? Others catch harmful caterpillars. Some of the smallest wasps thrust their eggs into the bodies of our garden pests. Then the tiny babies bore through the insect and kill it. They may be no larger than the size of the period at the end of this sentence.

Many ants are peaceful farmers or explorers. The terrible driver ants, however, eat everything in their path. Sometimes they enter jungle huts, and the natives flee for their lives. The driver ants chase away or kill every mouse and rat, insect and spider.

Why are some ants feared in the tropics?

Strange beetles, bugs and other insects live in the nests of many ants. They are usually not welcome, but they are not killed for some reason. When the ants are not looking, they steal some food, or even eat a few baby ants.

QUEEN   MALE   WORKER

There is much activity in an ant hill. Worker ants are pictured dragging a dead fly, a cocoon and a twig.

8. The Flies

How is a fly different from all other insects? When you catch a fly or mosquito, count its wings. The total may surprise you. All the other common insects have four wings, but the flies have only two. Instead of a second pair, they have a pair of knobs attached to the thorax. If these knobs are hurt, they cannot fly.

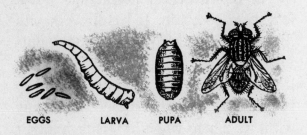

EGGS　　LARVA　　PUPA　　ADULT

The life cycle of the housefly includes four stages.

Do all flies have wings? One of the strangest flies lives in the fur of some animals. It has no wings, and runs around in the hair of sheep, goats and deer. It looks like a big flea. A few other wingless flies live in the feathers of some birds. Still another, a wingless crane fly, can sometimes be seen walking around on the snow. It looks like a spider, but has only six legs instead of the spider's eight. It is one of the first insects to come out in the spring.

TSETSE FLY

Can flies be dangerous? A few tropical flies are among the most dangerous of all insects. The anopheles mosquito carries malaria disease from one person to an-

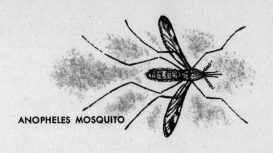

ANOPHELES MOSQUITO

other. The aedes mosquito carries yellow fever. The tsetse flies of Africa carry sleeping sickness. Houseflies may go right from a garbage pail to your dinner table. Doctors worked many years before they found ways to control these insects. Many of them caught the same diseases they were fighting.

How do some flies resemble other insects? Some flies look like other insects. Some are colored exactly like a bee. Others look like wasps or hornets. Some look like moths. But if you count the wings, you'll see that they are not wasps and bees at all — they are flies.

BEE FLY

How can a fly kill a spider? The bite of the black widow spider is very poisonous. But one tiny fly has learned to go right into this spider's web without getting caught. It lays its eggs on the spider's egg sac, and the maggots burrow inside. They eat the eggs of the spider. Then they fly away. Without these little flies there would probably be many more black widow spiders, so this fly, at least, can kill a spider.

Insects and Plants

Many kinds of insects cause galls on plants. A gall is a swelling. Some are made by flies. The mother fly lays her eggs in the stem of a plant. The stem begins to swell. The eggs hatch inside the swelling. Then the maggots live in their strange house.

What causes plant galls?

A few plants feed on insects. They are called insectivorous plants. The pitcher plant has leaves which are hollow and shaped like a flower vase. Rain water falls into them and makes a little puddle. Insects fall into the water and drown. Then the plant digests the insects, somewhat as

How do plants catch insects?

you digest the food you eat. Some pitcher plants are so large that they may trap frogs, lizards or even mice.

The sundew has sticky hairs on its leaves. Insects land on the leaves and get tangled in the sticky surface. Soon, like those in the pitcher plant, they are digested.

The milkweed catches insects, but it lets them go again. It has flowers with little traps in them. When an insect puts its foot in the trap, it is held fast. Then it struggles to get free. Finally the trap breaks off, and the insect flies away with it. Then when it visits another milkweed, grains of pollen in the trap fall out on the new blossom, so the milkweed can make its seeds.

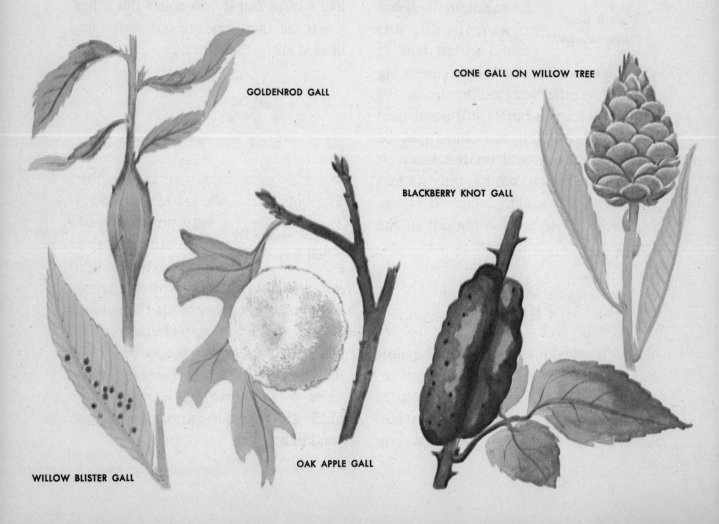

GOLDENROD GALL

CONE GALL ON WILLOW TREE

BLACKBERRY KNOT GALL

OAK APPLE GALL

WILLOW BLISTER GALL

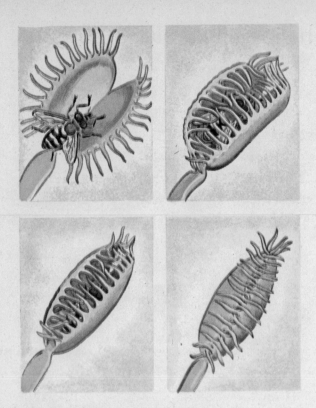

The Venus's-flytrap catches an insect.

Some plants even live inside the bodies

What plants live inside of insects? of insects. One fungus attacks houseflies and kills them. Another kind attacks caterpillars. Bacteria, which are so small that you need a microscope to see them, kill many others. Without these little plants, there would be even more insects in the world than there are now.

Many insects are useful in carrying

How do insects scatter seeds? seeds of plants. Small hooks on the seeds may catch in the hairs on the body of a fly or bee. Then the seed is carried through the air as the insect flies away. Later it drops off and starts a new plant. Some insects take seeds to their nests in the ground. The seeds may grow, starting a new plant right in the middle of the nest.

An insect stuck in the hairs of a sundew plant

One of the most interesting seeds is the

What is a Mexican jumping bean? Mexican jumping bean. This is a seed which contains a small caterpillar. This little insect chews away at the inside of the seed. It changes position every few minutes. Every time it moves, the seed rolls around, just as you can roll a big box by moving around inside it. Finally the caterpillar turns into a little moth. Then it flies away to lay its eggs in new seeds.

Fossils and Prehistoric Insects

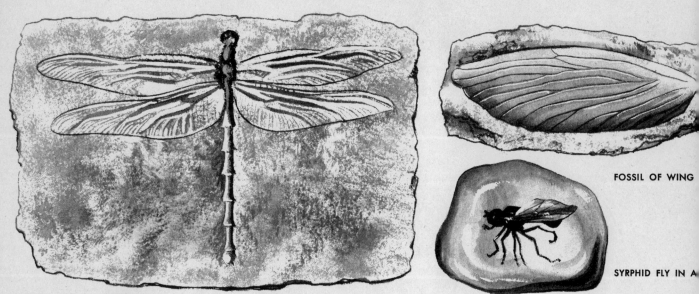

FOSSIL OF WING

SYRPHID FLY IN A

DRAGONFLY IN LIMESTONE

How are insect fossils made? If an insect, usually a large one, lands in soft mud or clay, it may get stuck there and eventually die. Frequently, the insect becomes completely buried in the mud, which may later turn into rock. When the insect wastes away, it leaves a natural print, or mold, of its body. Then, when the rock is broken, a picture-outline of the insect may be seen. Such prints and molds are known as "fossils."

What is an amber fossil? One of the most interesting insect fossils is the "amber fossil." Many kinds of trees, such as pines and spruces, have a sticky material known as resin. You may find it on the bark and trunk. Flies, ants, wasps and other insects often get tangled in this resin. More of it flows over them, covering them with a clear coating. Later this resin changes and hardens, becoming a substance known as amber. If there are insects inside, they will be preserved for millions of years by the hard material.

How old are some insect fossils? No one can be sure just when the first insects lived on this earth. Scientists have found insect fossils about 240 million years old. Some day they may find some that are still older. It is as interesting to hunt for fossil insects as it is to collect modern ones.

How large were prehistoric insects? If you could go backward about one million years, you would come to the days of the first cave man. Go back about 100 million years and you would see great dinosaurs. Go back still more, and you would see insect monsters. They would be even bigger than

SNAKE FLY IN SHALE

Many of the smaller insects survived. Their descendants still crawl and fly around today. So you see that insects have been on earth a long time. Many scientists feel that they will still be here when all other animal life is gone.

Could insects get as large as people? Could there possibly be a giant insect somewhere the size of a human being? Scientists do not think so. Animals which are very large need some kind of blood system to carry oxygen to all parts of the body. Insects have blood, but it doesn't carry oxygen. The spiracles and air tubes are fine for a small insect, but they just wouldn't work for an insect the size of a man. Besides, a man-sized insect would not have any bones inside, any more than the small ones do. So it would have to have a heavy jacket of armor for strength. Such armor would make it too slow and clumsy.

The more we look at the world of insects, the more interesting it is. We can see tiger beetles with long hairs on their feet so they won't sink into the sand of the dunes where they live. We can watch "slug caterpillars" that seem to move along like a little bulldozer. Gold beetles look as if they were made of pure gold. Tumblebugs roll little balls of material along like children making a snowman. Water pennies look like coins crawling slowly along the bottom of a stream.

the Goliath beetle or the giant walking stick. Cockroaches as big as saucers would run over the ground. Insects which look like giant dragonflies would sail through the air like model airplanes. Their wings would be more than two feet across — almost seven times larger than many of our common dragonflies today!

Why did the giant insects disappear? The great insects lived at a time when much of the earth was warm and food was easy to find. The many plants grew so thickly that they formed great heaps of plant material. This was later compressed and hardened into coal. After the coal-forming period, the land grew cold and dry. Many insects died in the harsh climate. Perhaps they died from other causes, too. Scientists are still trying to find the reasons, like detectives solving a mystery millions of years old.

Collecting Insects

You can make an insect collection of your own, which is one of the best ways to get to know the insects.

What do you need for an insect collection?

You will need these things:

(1) A magnifying glass.

(2) A pair of tweezers.

(3) A few dozen pins. (Regular insect pins are best. Perhaps a biology teacher can help you get some. If not, you may have to use common pins.)

(4) A box with a tight cover, such as a cigar box or a candy box.

(5) A piece of thick cardboard, cut to fit exactly into the bottom of the box. (With this, pins may be stuck in easily.)

(6) A killing jar. (This should have a tight lid. A pint-size jar will be fine. Put a crumpled piece of paper towel in the bottom, wet it with a few drops of cleaning fluid and force a circle of cardboard into the jar a little above the paper so that the insect cannot touch the damp paper. Keep the jar tightly closed when you are not using it.)

After you catch an insect, put it in the bottle for five minutes. It will quiet down right away. When it is still, take it out with the tweezers.

To keep your insect in good condition, carefully stick a pin through its thorax or chest from the top. Push the pin down until the pinhead is about one quarter of an inch above the insect's back. Beetles should have the pin stuck through the right wing. Put a small label on the pin, telling where and when you found the insect. If you know its name, put this on another label.

How should insects be mounted?

Stick the pin into the soft cardboard bottom of the box, and you'll be able to look at the insect whenever you wish. Always handle it with care after it is dry.

You can mount tiny insects, too. Glue them to one corner of a three-cornered piece of paper. Then push your pin through the center of the paper.

Butterflies and moths should have the wings spread. Do this as soon as possible after collecting them. Don't let them dry out. Spread the wings flat on a piece of soft wood, one at a time, until all four wings are out straight. Hold them in place with strips

How should butterflies and moths be mounted?

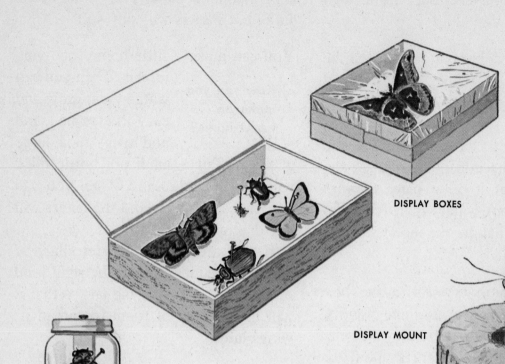

DISPLAY BOXES

DISPLAY MOUNT

DISPLAY JARS

MOUNTING BOARD

MAGNIFYING GLASS

KILLING JAR

of waxed paper. Never put pins through the wings.

If an insect gets hard and dry, it can be

How can dry insects be softened?

relaxed and softened with steam from an iron. Place it in a saucer and let the steam from the iron point right at the insect. Or put it on a piece of wire screen over hot water. In a few minutes you can handle the insect without breaking it.

Put a few moth crystals in the box

How can your collection be protected from other insects?

every three months. These are the same crystals used to protect winter clothing when it is stored away in the spring. Then other insects won't get in and eat up your collection. You can also keep insects in tiny bottles of alcohol. Regular rub-bing alcohol is good. Their colors soon fade, but insects will stay soft.

You can make a little home for living

How can you make an insect home?

insects. Then you can watch them grow and eat. Put some sand and twigs in a large glass jar. Put a small pill bottle filled with water in the sand. Then you can put leaves in the jar and the leaves will not dry up.

If you are raising a caterpillar, be sure you feed it plenty of the right kind of leaves. Use a good big jar, so that it will have plenty of room to spread its wings later.

You can make a little insect aquarium.

How can you keep water insects?

Fill a goldfish bowl half full of water. Put in a few pebbles and weeds for hiding places. Keep it out of bright light or the

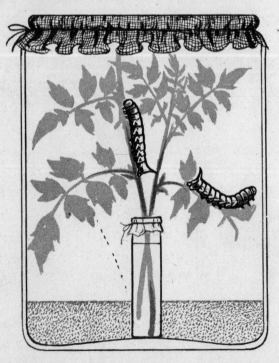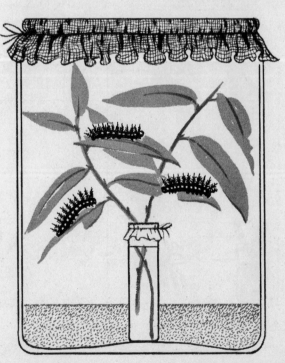

A jar with some water, a little sand and a covering made of plain gauze make a comfortable insect home.

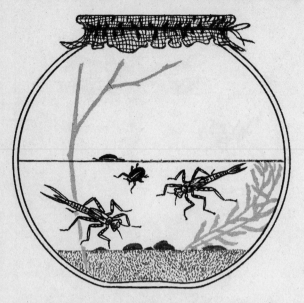

A bowl makes a comfortable home for water insects.

In a few weeks there were hundreds of baby mantises all over the room.

You can make a fine display with your insect collection. Beetles, grasshoppers and dragonflies can be mounted in special boxes and then hung on the wall of your room. Mounted butterflies and moths make interesting "pictures" to hang on walls or to give as gifts.

How can you display your collection?

To make a display case, find a large flat box, such as a writing paper box or candy box. Measure it and cut a piece of glass so that it will just fit over the box. Glue a picture hanger on the back of the box so it can be hung up later. Fill the box with cotton. It is a good idea to put some moth crystals in the cotton as protection against other insects.

How can you make a display case?

Place your insects carefully on the cotton. Press them down so they will stay in place. Butterflies and moths should be mounted while they are still soft and flexible. Then put the glass plate over them and seal it neatly around the edges with tape. A coat of black enamel over the box and the tape will seal all the small holes and make a good-looking display case.

Some companies make black cases with white cotton just for insects. These are called Riker mounts. A biology teacher will be able to tell you where you can get them. The teacher can also tell you about special kits for mounting insects in a dish of liquid plastic. When

water will turn green. Then you can put any water insect in your aquarium. Cover the top, because most water insects can fly.

Your pets will feed on a bit of liver or fish. Serve it to them on a pair of tweezers, or hang it in the water by a thread. Take out, in an hour, all food that they don't eat. In that way, decaying food will not foul the water.

You can find insect eggs and cocoons on twigs and dead leaves in winter. Keep them on the outside window sill until you are ready for them to hatch. The cold air will keep them fresh and healthy. If you keep them indoors where it is warm, they may hatch too soon.

How can eggs and cocoons be kept from hatching too soon?

A collector once brought in about a dozen praying mantis egg cases and left them on his desk. Then he forgot them.

An insect display box

the plastic hardens, you can take it out of the dish like an ice cube. Then it can be used as an ornament for your desk or as a gift.

A magnifying glass will help you learn

How can a magnifying glass help you?

much more about insects. It will show you many things too small to see without a lens. You may find an extra pair of eyes on the whirligig beetle, for instance. One is for seeing in the air, while the other is for looking under water. If you look in the center of a daisy, you'll see tiny black thrips. A close look at their legs shows that they walk around with feet that look like little balloons. Treehoppers look like prehistoric dinosaurs when they are seen under the magnifying glass.

In a few years, space ships may take men to Mars. They may even go beyond our own solar system. Some experts think they'll find strange new forms of life. But with a magnifying glass and a good sharp eye, we can stay home and find strange creatures of our own. Few animals that have ever lived are much stranger than the flies and beetles and bugs that live in the world right at our fingertips.